Behind
the
COUCH

Behind
the
COUCH

Mordicai Gerstein

To Elizabeth Gordon, who has done so much to
enrich the world with books, mine among them,
and
to my nephew, the real Zachary Harris
—M. G.

SRA Part No. R19983.08

Printed by SRA /McGraw-Hill.

Printed in the United States of America.

First Edition

The artwork for each picture is prepared using pen-and-ink.
This book is set in 16-point Berkeley Book.

Library of Congress Cataloging-in-Publication Data
Gerstein, Mordicai.
Behind the Couch / Mordicai Gerstein.—1st ed.
p.   cm.—(Hyperion Chapters)
Summary: When Zachary loses his oldest toy and first friend, he
searches for it behind the couch where he discovers a wonderful,
imaginary world.
ISBN 0-7868-0116-6 (trade)—ISBN 0-7868-1139-0 (pbk.)
ISBN 0-7868-2306-2 (lib. bdg.)
[1. Lost and found possessions—Fiction. 2. Imagination—
Fiction.] I. Title. II. Series.
PZ7.G325Bh   1996
[E]—dc20   95-41421

TABLE of CONTENTS

Chapter 1
WALLACE SLIPS

Wallace fell behind the couch. The top of the couch-back was the rim of the Grand Canyon, and Wallace, who had been speeding along it on a turbo-jet motorcycle, slipped, fell out of Zachary's hand, and was gone into the darkness between the couch and the wall.

"Zachary, dinner is ready."

"Just a minute, Mom, I have to get Wallace. He fell behind the couch."

Zachary hopped down to the side of

the couch and, on his knees, peered into the darkness between it and the wall. He could see nothing.

"Wallace, are you in there?" Zachary reached in his arm as far as he could. No Wallace. He must be just a little farther, thought Zachary, and he crawled in behind the couch.

One shoulder rubbed against the couch and the other rubbed the wall. All he could see was darkness. Crawling, he felt the furry, nubbly carpet under his palms. His hand closed over something cold, hard, and round. A marble. He slipped it into his pocket. And something else. A penny. I must be close to Wallace now, he thought, and he moved forward, feeling from side to side. His hand closed over a little toy car. He couldn't see it but he remembered it. It had disappeared long ago. But where was Wallace? The wooden feet at the back of the couch felt like bumpy tree roots. There were more of them than he would have thought.

"Wallace! Where are you?"

"Who's Wallace?" a voice answered. It didn't sound like Wallace's. In fact, being a stuffed pig, Wallace couldn't speak at all. Zachary, changing his voice, did Wallace's talking for him. Wallace was Zachary's oldest toy and first friend. They still slept together almost every night, but these days Zachary ususally played with his construction trucks, his giant Lego set, and his racing cars that could be transformed into spaceships. It was rare that, like today, Wallace was involved in Zachary's adventures.

But if it wasn't Wallace's voice that had answered him, whose was it?

"Who's there?" Zachary asked, his heart beating a little faster.

"You're there" said the voice. "I'm here!" It was familiar, though definitely not Wallace's. "Have some pistachios."

Zachary realized he could stand, and now there was just enough light for him to see the odd figure before him.

Chapter 2
UNCLE YANKLE

"Uncle Yankle!" said Zachary. "What are you doing here?"

"Everybody's gotta be someplace," said his uncle Yankle.

Uncle Yankle lived in an apartment in Baltimore, a city far from Zachary's. But here he was, sitting on a little hill in the carpet. He looked like an oversize teddy bear. His fleecy white hair looked like escaping stuffing, with more of it peeking over the top of his pajama shirt. He wore a faded bathrobe and old leather slippers.

"How's your mother?" he asked.

"She's fine, but what are you doing here?"

"When I was your age," said his uncle, "I used to jump up on the roof and pick stars out of the sky to eat for breakfast with milk and sugar. Talk about crunchy!"

"What's that got to do with your being here?" Zachary had heard this story each time his uncle came to visit.

"Now I'm old," continued Uncle Yankle, "and I can't jump up on the roof. But I can still climb up on my couch to water my hanging begonia—and *that's* when I dropped my glasses. The glasses I use to find my other glasses. I looked behind the couch, and guess what? I dropped my keys: house key, car key, bicycle key, piano key, tur-key, and mon-key." He chuckled a hoarse chuckle. "So I crawled behind the couch, and here I am. How's your father?"

"He's fine, but why are you behind *our* couch?" asked Zachary, "and not in Baltimore, behind yours?"

"If you crawl far enough behind *any* couch, you get to the same place. This place."

Zachary looked around. They were in a kind of forest. The trees were shaped like towering lamps or table or chair legs. Some were carved with curlicues, fruit, and animals. Looking up, Zachary saw that instead of leaves there were lampshades of all shapes and sizes. The lamps gave off a soft light. Above these a dark blue sky studded with fat star-shaped stars, ringed planets, and several moons, all of which looked like the stuck-on glow-in-the-dark ones in Zachary's room. Underfoot, the carpet, with its endless Oriental designs, went off in every direction.

"I'm not sure I understand," said Zachary.

"So have some pistachios and tell me what *you're* looking for." Uncle Yankle always had a pocket full of pistachios. Zachary took some.

"I lost Wallace, my pig."

"Wallace is perhaps a purple pig?"

"You saw him?"

"Saw him? We chatted for half an hour. We laughed, we cried, we sang songs, we tickled each other. He said to me, 'If you see Zachary, tell him good-bye.' He was going that way." Uncle Yankle pointed off through the trees. "He was riding an old duck pull-toy, the kind that goes *quackquackquack* . . ."

"But Wallace is just a stuffed pig," said Zachary. "He can't talk."

"Really?" said Uncle Yankle. "I could hardly get a word in. Things lost behind the couch change. Look."

Here and there, Zachary saw drifting balls of gray fluff as big as sheep. Uncle Yankle held out his hand to one. Timidly, it came closer.

"Come, sweetheart," said Uncle Yankle, "have some lint." It snuffed up what was held out, and when Uncle Yankle blew at the creature, it floated away.

"Yes," said the old man, "they're dust balls, gentle creatures. When they get big enough, they begin to move around, grazing on lint, bits of thread, whatever they can find. Well," he sighed, getting to his feet, "if you don't look, you don't find." He took Zachary's hand and they started through the furniture-leg forest.

Zachary heard a flapping, pitter-pat sound coming closer.

"What's that?" he asked, gripping his uncle's hand.

"Stand back!" said Yankle, "Or they'll run right over you!"

Hopping frantically through the trees, slippers of all shapes and sizes whizzed by and around them. Big and fluffy, flat and floppy, pink, blue, red, green, gray, one shaped like a duck, another like a bunny, no two alike. They hurtled past and on down a hill.

"The slippers that get lost behind the couch go wild," said Uncle Yankle. "They meet others, they form herds."

"Do all lost things go wild?"

"Sure, keys, glasses—coins gather and multiply . . ."

"Even stuffed animals?"

". . . even yo-yos and paper clips."

They turned at the sound of running feet. Someone—or something—was coming their way.

Chapter 3
RALPHINE

A girl with long, crinkled black hair and skin the color of gingerbread skidded into the clearing.

"Have you seen a slipper run through here?" she asked, trying to catch her breath.

It was Ralphine. Zachary thought she was the prettiest girl in the third grade. He'd always been too shy to talk to her.

"We just saw about a thousand of them," said Zachary. "What did it look like?" She held up a slipper shaped like a bunny and

15

Zachary nodded. "One just like it tore through here a minute ago."

"You're Zachary from my class!" said Ralphine. "What are you doing behind my couch?"

"Well, see . . . ," said Zachary, "if you go far enough behind each couch, it's behind all couches . . . ," Zachary blushed, ". . . or something like that. I'm looking for a friend of mine. This is my uncle Yankle from Baltimore. He's looking for his glasses and keys."

"You have very pretty hair, young lady," said Uncle Yankle, shaking Ralphine's hand.

"This is really a coincidence, Zachary," said Ralphine. "I just met a stuffed purple pig that asked me if I knew you."

"That was Wallace!" said Zachary. "He's

a . . . kind of . . . toy I *used* to have." Zachary was embarrassed at having the prettiest girl in his class know he still played with stuffed animals.

"He said if I saw you," continued Ralphine, "to tell you he was too old to play with you anymore, and that he was going into *politics*."

"How does he know about . . . politics?" asked Zachary. He wasn't sure what it was himself.

"Whoops!" yelped Uncle Yankle "Look out! The wild cars are chasing the slippers!"

They heard an angry, buzzing whine and the flustered pit-patting slippers were back, hopping like popcorn and pursued by hundreds of toy cars and trucks. The carpet swarmed with them. There were race cars and space cars, transformers and fire trucks, Batmobiles and Barbie cars, and in the middle of all of them, a large orange tabby cat seemed to be chasing everything.

"There's my old toy school bus!" shouted Zachary, pointing at a yellow plastic thing careening after a green slipper. It had been lost and forgotten years ago.

In a moment cars and slippers were gone. There was only the orange tabby, batting and

chewing on something it had caught.

"*That's my slipper!*" screamed Ralphine.

The cat looked at her with big green eyes, the quivering slipper held securely beneath its paws.

"Do you have any proof?" asked the cat, each word precise and neat as its pink tongue. "A sales slip, perhaps? A receipt?"

"WOW!" said Zachary. All the fairy tales and cartoons of talking animals hadn't

prepared him for the thrill of the reality. "Can you *really* talk?" he asked the cat.

"Peterpiperpickedapeckofpickledpeppers," said the cat, turning its green gaze onto Zachary. "Your turn."

"Peterpopperpookedapippa . . . ah . . ." Zachary stammered to a halt. This cat, he thought, speaks better than *I* do.

"Here's my proof!" said Ralphine, holding up her foot with the other slipper. Seeing its mate, the captive slipper squeaked and leapt free. It dashed to Ralphine and she quickly slipped her foot into it.

"We missed you!" she said, looking down and rubbing the two slippers together.

"Rats!" said the cat.

"Do you live here?" Zachary asked the cat, who was now licking its tail.

"Here, there, and everywhere," answered the cat. "I come behind the couch to sharpen my claws," it clawed the carpeting back and forth, "and to chase things. I just chased a squealing purple pig all over the woods. What fun!"

"Wallace!" said Zachary. "Did you hurt him?"

"Of course not," said the cat, "though to hear him shriek you'd think I had. I just chewed on his tail a little and let him go."

"Which way did he go?" Zachary asked the cat.

"Who knows?" said the cat, "maybe that way or maybe *that* way!" The cat's ears flicked straight up. "Or maybe that way." Its head eased forward and it froze, tail switching side to side. Something behind a tree was moving.

Chapter 4
CAPTURING the KEYS

The cat pounced and an odd kind of daddy longlegs raced madly around everyone's feet. The cat was right behind it. It took a moment for Zachary to realize that it was a pair of glasses running on the arms that hook over your ears. Then a jingling thing was chasing both the cat and the glasses.

"You get the glasses!" Uncle Yankle yelled to the cat. "And kids, help me corner my keys! Careful! They can be nasty when cornered." The jangling keys zigzagged between their legs. Zachary grabbed for them but missed. They were quick, but at the base of a chair-leg tree Zachary, Ralphine, and Uncle Yankle surrounded them. The keys hopped up and down, jingling fiercely.

"Stand back!" said Uncle Yankle. "Don't antagonize them." The cat paraded up to him with the helpless spectacles held gently in its mouth.

"Thank you," he said to the cat. He wiped the glasses with a large white handkerchief, put them on, blew his nose, and then turned to the quivering key ring.

"All right, calm down, calm down now, and come to Uncle Yankle . . . come on." He slowly turned his back and, looking over his shoulder, held open the pocket of his bathrobe. "Come on . . . come to uncle . . . ," he crooned, patting his pocket. The keys jingled uncertainly, unable to decide.

"Come, sweethearts, come home to uncle . . ."

With a sudden hop and a breathtaking leap, the keys arced into Uncle Yankle's pocket. Zachary and Ralphine cheered, and Uncle Yankle took a formal bow.

"Zachary," he said, "good luck with Wallace. Ralphine, it was a pleasure to meet you. Good luck with your slipper."

"You're leaving?" Zachary asked. "How come?"

"When I was your age, I used to jump up on the . . ."

"I know all that!" said Zachary.

". . . also," said his uncle, "I left the bath

running. You should all come visit me in Baltimore."

"What kinds of cat food do they have there?" asked the cat.

"Well, we have Sumptuous Seafood Delight, we have Feline Picnic Treats . . ."

"I'll come now," said the cat. "It's dinner-time."

"Delighted," said Uncle Yankle. He kissed one of Zachary's cheeks, pinched the other, and gave him a handful of pistachios. "Give my love to your mother and father." With keys jingling, he and the cat sauntered into the woods.

"But Uncle Yankle . . . ," Zachary called after them, "what if we get lost?"

"Pencils get lost behind the couch," his uncle called back, "pennies, purple pigs, but *not* people!" The old man waved and disappeared among the trees. Zachary felt abandoned.

"Which way do you think we should go?" he asked Ralphine. She shrugged. They both looked at the lamp and furniture-leg forest that surrounded them. Grazing dust balls drifted here and there. A chain of paper clips slithered over the carpet. Far off, a pair of red suspenders ran through the woods like a deranged octopus, followed a moment later by the orange tabby.

"That cat may never get to Baltimore," said Zachary.

"Listen," said Ralphine, cupping her ear.

"It sounds like singing," said Zachary. "It's over that way." They started toward the sound.

Chapter 5
BEVERLY

After a moment Ralphine took Zachary's hand.

"Don't look back," she whispered. "We're being followed." Something was flopping along behind them. Zachary took a deep breath and whirled around. There stood a bedraggled, plaid stuffed duck.

"*Bowwow*," it said sadly, in a voice like someone holding their nose. "*Bowwow.*"

"What are you doing?" Zachary asked it.

"I'm *pretending* to be a cocker spaniel

29

scaring cats," said the duck. "But I'm *actually* a stuffed duck. Are you cats or bears?"

"We're kids," said Zachary.

"BEVERLY!" shouted Ralphine.

"RALPHINE!" cried the duck, "you're all grown-up! Why did you drop me behind the couch?"

"I was five and it was an accident!" said Ralphine, hugging the stuffed animal. "But I never forgot you!"

"Do you know a purple pig named Wallace?" Zachary asked Beverly.

"Of course," said Beverly. "We're engaged."

"You mean . . . to be married?" gasped Zachary.

"It was love at first sight," said Beverly. "Purple's my favorite color."

"Where is he?"

"In the Valley of Stuffed Animals. It's just over Lost Coin Hill." Beverly pointed. "Look!"

Through the trees Zachary saw a hill that glowed in the soft light.

"Come on!" said Ralphine, taking Zachary's hand. They began to run toward the hill, which seemed to grow bigger as they got closer. Underfoot the carpet was scattered with pennies, then pennies and nickels, and then nickels and dimes. All around they heard the murmer of tiny voices: ". . . four times four is sixteen, five times four is twenty, six times four is twenty-four . . ."

"They're multiplying!" shouted Zachary. He scooped up a handful of coins and saw, as the tiny presidents on them chanted the times tables, pennies turn into nickels and nickels become dimes and then overflow his cupped hands. As he and Ralphine reached the base of the mountain that now towered over them, the coins had become quarters and silver dollars. They lay thicker and deeper underfoot and the going became slippery and difficult.

"We're RICH!" shouted Zachary, flinging

handfuls of coins into the air over his head. "Ouch!" he yelped a moment later as they fell back. "They're heavy and they hurt!"

"RICH, RICH, RICH!" echoed Ralphine. They both threw themselves spread-eagle on the mountainside and rolled and slid through the shining silvery disks.

"RICH! RICH! RICH!" screamed Beverly,

33

doing somersaults. "What does RICH mean?" she asked.

"We can buy anything in the whole world!" said Zachary.

"YES!" crowed Beverly. "Let's buy the whole world!" She thought for a moment. ". . . but where would we put it?"

Zachary and Ralphine slid to their knees and filled their pockets. "That's about all I can carry," said Zachary, holding up his pants, which were now weighted down with coins.

"Me, too," said Ralphine. Her sweater pockets banged against her knees.

But when the three of them started up the mountain, the coins kept mumbling and multiplying in their pockets and, except for Beverly, they just kept slipping back. After a minute or so, neither Zachary nor Ralphine could stand up or even move.

"What'll we do?" moaned Zachary.

Ralphine sighed. "I guess we'll just have to leave these here," she said as she dumped her coins. Zachary nodded and did the same.

"FOLLOW ME!" sang Beverly and they continued their climb.

At the very top they sank, exhausted, and looked down into a valley surrounded by mountains of wrinkled carpet. Hundreds of little figures milled about and, through the drone of chanted multiplication tables, the faint sound of singing wafted up to them.

"THE VALLEY OF STUFFED ANIMALS!" yelled Beverly, and started sliding down the mountain. Ralphine grabbed her tail and slid after her.

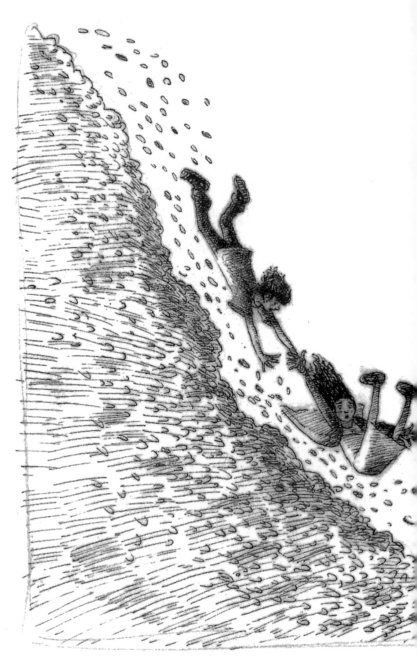

"Ralphine! Wait!" yelled Zachary. He caught her hand and was pulled down with her.

They started slowly but quickly picked up speed until they were careening and bouncing down a flashing river of silver. There was just wind and blur and the hissing, tinkling roar of falling coins.

Chapter 6
THE VALLEY of STUFFED ANIMALS

They skidded to a stop on level ground in a shower of pennies. Zachary caught his breath. His ears rang with a silvery jingle.

"Are you guys real or stuffed?" asked a green teddy bear, stepping from behind a tree.

"They're real," answered Beverly. "I'm stuffed."

"We don't need *real* kids here," said a pink penguin, one of half a dozen stuffed animals that now surrounded them. "We have our own stuffed animal country here."

"That's right," said the bear. "We even have a president and everything!"

"YAAY FOR THE PRESIDENT!" cheered all the animals.

"What is a president?" asked Beverly.

"It's a stuffed purple pig," said the penguin. "Everybody knows that."

"Is his name Wallace?" asked Zachary.

"If it is, I'm engaged to him," said Beverly.

"Then you'll be First Duck!" said a giraffe. "HURRY! The president's going to make a speech!"

"What's a speech?" asked Beverly as the animals went skipping off. The children hurried after them. The singing and cheering were louder now.

The carpet dipped and formed a stadium-shaped bowl filled with stuffed animals of every kind, all chattering and singing. Some played patty-cake and peekaboo. In the center, lit by spotlights fastened to the dark blue sky, was a vast coffee table. A purple pig hopped onto it and began to tap-dance. All the animals cheered.

"That's him!" Zachary said to Ralphine. "That's Wallace! I didn't know he could tap-dance."

Chapter 7
HAIL TO THE CHIEF

"My dear friends!" Wallace shouted in his squeaky voice. "Our national anthem!" There was the sound of a toy piano and a kazoo, and all the animals began to sing:

"Happy birthday to us!

Happy birthday to us!

Happy birthday to everybody,

Happy birthday to us! YAAAAAAY!"

All around them balloons flew up and attached themselves to the sky.

"Wallace!" shouted Zachary. "It's me!

Zachary!" It was suddenly very quiet. Wallace looked up.

"Zachary who?" asked Wallace.

"Zachary Harris. I came looking for you."

"The Zachary Harris who has a plastic pterodactyl with a cobweb on its nose hanging from the ceiling of his room?"

"Yes, Wallace, it's me!"

"What do you want, Zachary? I'm kind of busy right now."

"I came looking for you, to bring you home."

"Don't you know we had an election here? Don't you know I'm president of all the stuffed animals in the *entire universe*?"

"YAAAAY President Wallace!" screamed all the animals. More balloons flew up.

"I never thought you'd be president," said Zachary.

"You thought I was just a *baby* toy, *didn't* you?" said Wallace.

"What do you do as president?" asked Zachary.

"The usual stuff. Tap-dance, stand on my head, and, of course, make tons of speeches. Stay here, Zachary. Pretend to be a teddy bear and have fun all the time!"

"Doing what?" asked Zachary.

"Playing tag with the slippers and cars, never going to school, and having a birthday party every day. Every day is everybody's birthday here!"

"HOOOORAAAY!" shouted all the animals. They started to sing the national anthem again.

"What about tea parties?" asked Ralphine.

"Every day!" said Wallace. "Both plain and fancy."

"I'll stay!" cried Ralphine. "Let's stay," she said to Zachary.

"I can't," said Zachary. "I have my violin lessons and the soccer league and school and video games. Besides, it's dinnertime and I'm getting hungry."

"Have some stars," said Wallace. "I hear they're very crunchy."

"Actually," said Ralphine, "I should go, too.

My little brother will get into my room and mess up all my stuff."

"Please come back, Wallace," said Zachary. "I miss you."

"Then why did you drop me behind the couch?"

"YES!" the animals all shouted. "WHY DID YOU DROP US BEHIND THE COUCH?"

Zachary felt a little uneasy. Ralphine took his hand.

"It was just an accident," she said to Wallace.

"Zachary," said Wallace, "do you know what stuffed animals are stuffed with?"

"Cotton?" said Zachary.

"FEELINGS!" said Wallace.

"And also FEATHERS!" shouted Beverly.

"FEELINGS AND FEATHERS!" shouted all the animals.

"Do you think," continued Wallace, "that I haven't noticed you rarely play with me anymore?"

"HARDLY EVER!" shouted a calico mouse.

"Sometimes you don't even sleep with me."

"ALMOST NEVER!" shouted a plush

bunny. Wallace held up his arms and the animals quieted.

"It's because," said Wallace, "I can't play soccer, isn't it?"

"SOCCER! BOOOOOOO!" shouted all the animals.

"No!" yelled Zachary. "Soccer's fun, but that's different! Come home with me Wallace. Please? I love you."

There was complete silence.

Chapter 8
MACARONI and CHEESE

"I love you, too," said Wallace. He hopped off the coffee table. "Let's go home."

"THEN WHO WILL BE OUR PRESIDENT?" shouted the animals. Some started to cry.

"And who will be First Duck?" asked Beverly.

"Excuse me," said a familiar voice. "I hate to interrupt, but did anyone see a pair of red suspenders run through here?" It was Uncle Yankle.

"Mr. Yankle," said Wallace, "how would you like to be president of all the stuffed animals in the universe?"

"How would I like it?" Uncle Yankle smiled. "To tell you the truth, I'd be TICKLED PINK!"

"Are you real or stuffed?" asked the penguin.

"Half-and-half," said Uncle Yankle. "My father was a stuffed bunny, and I'm a teddy bear at heart."

"HOOORAYFORPRESIDENTYANKLE!" shouted everyone.

Uncle Yankle hopped onto the coffee table and started to tap-dance. Wallace took Zachary's hand.

"So long, guys," he said to all the animals.

"Give my love to your parents," Uncle

Yankle said, waving, "and tell them to come visit. I'm just behind the couch!" The crowd started singing "Happy Birthday" again.

"It's the only song they know," Wallace said as they started off. "Hi, Beverly. Are we still engaged?"

"Of course," said Beverly. "Purple's still my favorite color."

"Now I'm really hungry," said Zachary.

"Me, too," said Ralphine.

"I'm stuffed," said Beverly.

"Me, too," said Wallace. "There's really not much for you guys to eat here. Mostly old chewing gum—or sometimes a lint-covered lollipop or piece of marzipan."

"We're having macaroni and cheese for dinner," said Zachary to Ralphine. "Why don't you come over?"

"Yes," said Wallace, "Zachary thinks you're the prettiest girl in the class!" Ralphine and Zachary both blushed.

"I'd have to call home first," said Ralphine.

Wallace seemed to know the way. He led them through the trees among herds of dust balls, and over and around bumps in the carpet.

"Duck your head," said Wallace. "It's hands and knees from here."

They crawled into what became a dark tunnel that grew narrower till Zachary felt his shoulders scrape the couch on one side and the wall on the other. He picked up Wallace and crawled out from behind the couch.

"You have a nice house," said Ralphine, following him out into the living room. They could both smell the macaroni and cheese.

"Wash your hands, Zachary," said his mother from the kitchen. "Dinner is already on the table."

"Can Ralphine have dinner with us if her mom says it's OK?" asked Zachary.

"Who is Ralphine?" came his mother's voice from the kitchen.

"A girl from my class," answered Zachary. "Can she use the phone?"

"Is she here?" asked his mother, sticking her head out of the kitchen.

"Yes," said Zachary, "and so is Wallace. And President Yankle sends his love."

THE END

Mordicai Gerstein has written and illustrated many books for children, including *The Mountains of Tibet,* a 1987 *New York Times* Best Illustrated Book, and *The Shadow of a Flying Bird.* He is the illustrator of the Something Queer series, also published by Hyperion Books for Children. Mr. Gerstein lives in Massachusetts with his wife and daughter.